Understanding
TRAUMA, ABUSE AND ADDICTIONS

Harrison S. Mungal, Ph.D., PsyD

Understanding Trauma, Abuse, and Addictions

Copyright © 2023 Harrison S. Mungal

Contact author via email: hsmungal@hotmail.com
www.agetoage.ca,
www.harrisonmungal.com
Facebook: Harrison Mungal
Twitter: HarrisonandKathleen @HKrelationships,
AgetoAge @agetoagec
LinkedIn: Harrison Mungal, Ph.D., PsyD
YouTube: Harrison Mungal
Phone: 905-533-1334

ABOUT the
AUTHOR

Harrison holds two doctorate degrees, one in Clinical Psychology and the other in Philosophy in Social Work. He has two master's degrees, a master's degree in Social Work and a master's degree in Counselling. And a Bachelor's degree in Theology. He specializes in mental health, addictions, marriage and relationships, parenting, and family.

Harrison is considered one of the leading cognitive therapist workshop presenters. He wears many hats in supporting individuals, couples, families, and corporations. He has been a public speaker to over forty-two nations as a keynote speaker at conferences, seminars, and public events, as well as a speaker on several Radio and Television programs. He has written over twenty-five books. He is appreciated for the depth of his knowledge, great humour and passion for relationships, parenting, mental health, addictions, and other related life struggles.

Harrison utilizes a creative scientific-based approach to deliver compelling presentations that have granted him an excellent reputation. He has received several awards and recognitions from local police, mayors, community leaders, managers and directors, and families. He provides training and consultations to various community partners, including psychiatrists, medical doctors, social workers, nurses, police officers, firefighters and senior management teams.

Harrison has been involved in cognitive research to support individuals with addictions, psychosis, anxiety, and depression. He spearheaded several research studies on various themes, including music therapy and schizophrenia, vaccinations for children under six years old, substance abuse and addiction in the food service industry, and Thought Developmental Practice (TDP). His research on TDP with outpatient provided diversion methods to support substance abuse and addictions, anxiety, and depression under the supervision of the chief of psychiatry, Dr. David Koczerginski.

Harrison has over twenty-one years of professional experience working with diverse populations, including seventeen years in mental health and more than ten years as a psychotherapist. These diverse populations include youth and adult offenders, communities impacted by Acquired Brain Injuries, refugees, war victims, and those needing crisis-based support in various settings, i.e., liaison with police, hospitals, community agencies, and inpatient mental health settings.

Harrison specializes in evidence-based therapies, including Cognitive Behavioural Therapy (CBT), Cognitive Processing Therapy (CPT), Dialectical Behavioural Therapy (DBT), Thought Developmental Practice (TDP), Acceptance and Commitment Therapy (ACT), Interpersonal therapy (IPT), Motivational Interviewing Techniques, Grounding Techniques, Integrative Eclectic Therapy, Humanistic Experiential Therapy, Interpersonal Therapy, Supportive Therapy, Exposure Therapy, Visual Therapy, Psychodynamic Therapy.

INTRODUCTION

Trauma, abuse, and addictions often arrive at the intersection of pain and survival. They are not simply clinical labels but deeply human experiences—layers of memory, emotion, and adaptation that speak to the resilience of those who have suffered and endured.

In this journey of exploration, we do not begin with pathology. We begin with empathy. Behind every addiction is a story—often one of unmet needs, relational ruptures, or silent suffering. Behind every trauma is a nervous system trying to protect itself, a person doing their best to stay afloat in overwhelming waters.

Psychology teaches us that healing unfolds in connection. Recovery is possible not because someone is "strong enough," but because someone is finally seen. Through safe therapeutic relationships, through education and emotional insight, we can begin to untangle the knots of shame, fear, and despair that trauma and abuse leave behind. We can offer language to those whose experiences were once unspeakable, and remind them: their pain has meaning, and their healing has value.

This work invites clinicians, survivors, and caregivers alike to view these issues not as isolated conditions, but as interconnected expressions of human distress and adaptive coping. And most of all, it invites compassion—not just for others, but for ourselves.

Table of Contents

UNDERSTANDING
TRAUMA, ABUSE, AND ADDICTIONS

Traumas, abuses, and mental illnesses are unfortunately prevalent in our society, and they can occur at any stage of life, affecting people of all ages, genders, ethnicity, and backgrounds. The effects of these negative experiences can be long-lasting, and they can significantly impact a person's physical and emotional health and relationships with others. For many people, the road to healing can be difficult, and it often involves overcoming stigmas and criticisms associated with these issues.

Different types of traumas, abuses, and mental illnesses affect each person differently. There are criticisms and stigmas surrounding these issues, which demand different types of treatment and support. Understanding and education will create a compassionate and empathetic mind to support those who need recovery in the aftermath of such experiences.

Traumas, abuses, and mental illnesses can have significant and wide-ranging impacts on a person's life. The physical effects of these negative experiences can include chronic pain, fatigue, headaches, digestive issues, and even an increased risk of developing chronic illnesses such as heart disease and diabetes. These physical symptoms can further impact a person's mental health, exacerbating symptoms of anxiety and depression and causing feelings of isolation and hopelessness.

The social impact of these issues can also be profound. Traumas and abuses can alter a person's trust in others, leading to difficulties forming and maintaining relationships. Those who have experienced trauma or abuse may feel ashamed or stigmatized, leading them to withdraw from social situations and further impacting their mental health.

Mental illnesses can have significant social impacts. Symptoms such as anxiety and depression, including mood swings and psychosis, can lead to social withdrawal, isolation, and a decreased ability to enjoy once-pleasurable activities. In severe cases, mental illness can also impact a person's ability to work or maintain other critical social roles, leading to financial instability and further exacerbating symptoms.

These experiences can lead to helplessness, hopelessness, and despair and interfere with a person's ability to lead a happy, fulfilling life. For many, the road to recovery can be long and challenging, involving therapy, medication, and other forms of support. However, it's important to note that recovery is possible, and there is hope for those who have experienced traumas, abuses, and mental illnesses. With the proper support and treatment, individuals can learn to manage their symptoms, heal their hurts, and rebuild their lives.

For those who have experienced trauma or abuse, it's essential to know that we are not alone. Many resources are available to help with healing, including therapy, support groups, and other forms of support. It's also important to remember that healing is a journey and that taking things one step at a time is okay.

Traumas can occur in various settings, from personal to public. At home, traumas can be domestic violence, neglect, or emotional abuse. These experiences can leave individuals feeling unsafe and unsupported. It can have a long-lasting impact on their mental health. Children who experience trauma in the home may struggle with trust issues, self-esteem, and social relationships well into adulthood.

In schools, traumas can occur through bullying, harassment, or discrimination. Children who are bullied may experience anxiety, depression, and post-traumatic stress disorder (PTSD).

Sexual abuse involves sexual contact without a person's consent, including unwanted touching, sexual assault, or rape. It can result in various physical and psychological symptoms, including depression, anxiety, PTSD, and substance abuse. Victims of sexual abuse by authority figures such as teachers and coaches may experience shame and guilt, making it difficult for them to come forward and seek help. Those who their next-door neighbour abuses may feel embarrassed to share with their family or the family of the neighbours.

In the workplace, traumas can occur through harassment, discrimination, or physical harm. These experiences can lead to feelings of anxiety, depression, and PTSD. Traumas can lead to physical health problems, including hypertension, cardiac-related issues, and diabetes. Workplace traumas can also lead to decreased productivity and increased absenteeism, impacting the individual and the entire organization.

In the community, traumas can occur through violence, natural disasters, or other traumatic events. These experiences can significantly impact a person's mental health, leading to feelings of anxiety, depression, and PTSD. It is important to note that trauma doesn't just affect individuals, but it can also have a broader impact on society. Communities that experience high levels of trauma may struggle with increased crime rates, poverty, and mental health issues. This, in turn, can lead to decreased economic opportunities and decreased quality of life for individuals living in those communities.

Abuses come in many different forms, each with its damaging effects. Physical abuse involves using physical force, such as hitting or pushing, to cause harm to another person. It can lead to physical injuries and emotional trauma, resulting in depression, anxiety, and post-traumatic stress disorder (PTSD).

On the other hand, emotional abuse involves using words, actions, or behaviours to manipulate, intimidate, gaslight, stonewall, ice or even belittle another person. It can include verbal diarrhea, insults, humiliation, or threats, resulting in low self-esteem, depression, and anxiety.

Neglect occurs when a caregiver fails to provide for a child or dependent adult's basic needs, such as food, shelter, and medical care. It can result in many physical and emotional problems, including malnutrition, poor hygiene, and developmental delays.

Financial abuse involves the misuse or control of a person's finances, such as stealing money or assets, coercing someone to give up their money, or forcing them to sign over control of their finances. It can lead to financial problems and loss of independence and exacerbate mental health issues.

All these forms of abuse can have significant adverse effects on a person's mental health and, in some cases, can even lead to long-term physical health problems. It's important to remember that abuse can happen to anyone, regardless of their age, gender, race, or socioeconomic status.

Abuse can also occur in relationships, and it can take various forms, such as emotional abuse, sexual abuse, and physical abuse. In some cases, it may involve both the victim and the perpetrator being involved in the abuse, with both parties being affected by mental health issues.

In the workplace, abuse can occur in different forms, such as bullying, harassment, and discrimination. This type of abuse can significantly impact an individual's mental health, leading to stress, anxiety, and depression, and can cause the person to develop low self-esteem and self-worth.

The effects of abuse can be long-lasting and profoundly impact an individual's physical and mental health. For many people, the abuse results can persist long after the abuse has ended, leading to difficulties in forming and maintaining healthy relationships and causing trust issues and emotional instability.

If you or someone you know is experiencing abuse,

it's essential to seek help as soon as possible. This can include contacting local law enforcement, seeking counselling or therapy, or contacting a trusted friend or family member for support. Many resources are available for those who have experienced abuse, and it's important to know that help is available.

Mental illnesses are a significant concern that affects millions of people globally. They refer to a wide range of disorders that impact an individual's thinking, emotions, and behaviour, often leading to functional impairments.

Anxiety disorders are conditions where a person experiences persistent worry, fear, or apprehension. They can manifest in different forms, such as panic disorder, social anxiety disorder, or specific phobias. Anxiety disorders are associated with abnormal activity in the amygdala, a part of the brain responsible for processing emotions, leading to exaggerated responses to perceived threats. It is the fear of the unknown.

Mood disorders, including depression and bipolar disorder, are characterized by persistent changes in mood that affect an individual's ability to function. Depression is a mood disorder involving constant sadness, hopelessness, and loss of interest in activities once enjoyed. On the other hand, bipolar disorder involves periods of manic episodes characterized by feelings of euphoria, increased energy levels, and risky behaviour. Individuals can have grandiose ideas and function in a psychotic state. Mood disorders are associated with changes in the levels of neurotransmitters, including serotonin and dopamine, which regulate mood, pleasure, and reward.

Personality disorders are a group of mental illnesses that involve long-standing patterns of behaviours, thoughts, and emotions that differ from societal norms. Personality disorders are classified into three clusters: Cluster A, B, and C. Cluster A personality disorders include paranoid personality disorder, which involves odd and eccentric behaviour. Cluster B personality disorder has a borderline personality disorder which affects erratic and impulsive behaviour. And Cluster C personality disorders include avoidant personality disorder, which affects anxious and fearful behaviour. Personality disorders are associated with abnormalities in brain structure and functionality.

Schizophrenia is a severe mental illness that affects an individual's ability to think, feel, and behave clearly. Symptoms include delusions, hallucinations, disorganized speech, paranoia, and odd behaviours. Schizophrenia is associated with neurotransmitter abnormalities, such as dopamine, glutamate, and GABA, and brain structure and function.

Eating disorders, including anorexia nervosa, bulimia nervosa, and binge-eating disorders, are characterized by abnormal eating patterns that affect an individual's physical and mental health. Eating disorders are associated with abnormalities in brain structure and function, particularly in the areas responsible for reward and self-control.

Some specific individuals are more susceptible to these negative experiences than others. Understanding who is most vulnerable to these issues is crucial in preventing them from occurring and providing the necessary support and treatment to those affected.

Children are particularly vulnerable to traumas and abuses, as they are still developing and may not have the coping mechanisms necessary to deal with traumatic events. Children who experience abuse or neglect may be more likely to develop mental health issues later in life, including anxiety, depression, and post-traumatic stress disorder. It's essential to recognize the signs of abuse and neglect in children and take action to prevent further harm.

Women are at a higher risk of experiencing traumas and abuses, particularly sexual and domestic violence. World Health Organization reported that one in three women will experience physical or sexual violence in their lifetime. Women who experience abuse are more likely to develop mental health issues, including depression, anxiety, and post-traumatic stress disorder. Additionally, women who experience trauma or abuse during pregnancy may be at a higher risk of complications such as preterm birth and low birth weight.

Men can also experience traumas and abuses, but they may be less likely to report or seek help for these issues due to societal expectations of masculinity. Men who experience abuse may be more likely to develop substance abuse issues or engage in risky behaviours to cope. Creating a safe and supportive environment for men to seek help and address their mental health needs is essential.

Older adults are also vulnerable to traumas and abuses, particularly in long-term care facilities or from caregivers. Elder abuse can take many forms, including physical, emotional, and financial abuse. Older adults who experience abuse may be at a higher risk of developing mental health issues, including depression and anxiety. They may be more socially isolated, which can exacerbate these issues.

Recognizing that different groups may be affected differently by traumas, abuses, and mental illnesses is essential. The symptoms of depression may present differently in men than in women, and cultural differences may influence how individuals perceive and cope with traumatic events. Understanding these nuances is crucial in providing adequate support and treatment.

The physical effects of traumas, abuses and mental Illnesses can include chronic pain, fatigue, headaches, digestive issues, and an increased risk of developing chronic illnesses such as heart disease and diabetes. These physical symptoms can further impact a person's mental health, exacerbating symptoms of anxiety and depression and causing feelings of isolation and hopelessness.

The social impact of these issues can also be profound. Traumas and abuses can damage a person's trust in others, leading to difficulties forming and maintaining relationships. Those who have experienced trauma or abuse may feel ashamed or stigmatized, leading them to withdraw from social situations and further impacting their mental health.

Mental illnesses have significant social impacts. Anxiety, depression, mood swings and psychosis can lead to social withdrawal, isolation, and a decreased ability to enjoy once-pleasurable activities. In severe cases, mental illness can also impact a person's ability to work or maintain other critical social roles, leading to financial instability and further exacerbating symptoms. However, it's important to note that recovery is possible, and there is hope for those who have experienced traumas, abuses, and mental illnesses. With the proper support and treatment, individuals can learn to manage their symptoms, heal from their experiences, and rebuild their lives.

For individuals who have experienced trauma, abuse and mental illnesses, knowing that you are not alone is essential. Many resources are available to help you heal, including therapy, support groups, and other forms of support. It's also important to remember that healing is a journey and that taking things one step at a time is okay. With the proper treatment, individuals can learn to manage their symptoms and improve their overall quality of life.

One of the most significant obstacles to healing from traumas, abuses, and mental illnesses is the criticism and stigmas associated with these issues. Sadly, the experience of trauma, abuse, or mental illness is often met with a range of adverse reactions, including victim blaming, minimization of experiences, and the belief that a person should simply "get over it."

Victim blaming is a common criticism often arising when someone experiences a traumatic event or abuse. This criticism typically involves blaming the victim for the experience or suggesting that the person somehow caused or deserved the event. Victim blaming can be especially harmful because it can lead to feelings of shame and self-blame, hindering a person's ability to heal and recover.

Another criticism often arises in the context of traumas, abuses, and mental illnesses is the minimization of experiences. This criticism involves downplaying the severity of a person's experiences, suggesting that they are overreacting or exaggerating the event's impact. Depreciation can be especially harmful because it can lead a person to question the validity of their experiences, making it difficult for them to seek help and support.

There is a pervasive belief that individuals should simply "get over it" and move on from the event or experience. This criticism suggests that a person should be able to overcome the effects of trauma, abuse, or mental illness quickly without seeking professional help or support. This view can be particularly damaging because it can lead individuals to feel as though they are weak or inadequate for struggling with the impact of these negative experiences. When people think they are being blamed, minimized, or judged for their experiences, they are less likely to seek help or support. They may feel ashamed or embarrassed or believe there is no point in seeking help because no one will understand or accept them.

Recognizing that traumas, abuses, and mental illnesses are serious issues that can profoundly impact a person's life is crucial. It is essential to offer support and empathy to those who have experienced these adverse events and to recognize the bravery and strength it takes to confront and overcome these experiences. By reducing the stigma and criticism associated with these issues, we can create a more supportive and compassionate environment that encourages healing and recovery

TRAUMA

Trauma is an emotional reaction to a catastrophic occurrence that affects our psychological well-being. It includes accidents, abuses, war-related events, and natural disasters where our sensory nerves have formulated 'memory cards.' Any circumstances we have experienced physically or emotionally can be traumatic, which can be triggered by reoccurrences of similar or related incidents.

A traumatized individual may react in various ways, including shock, grief, or denial, which are familiar with short-term responses. However, when diagnosed with post-traumatic stress disorder (PTSD), the symptoms are more long-term related, which include nightmares, flashbacks, hypervigilance, lack of impulse control, lack of motivation, depression and anxiety, psychosis, fatigue, and instability in relationships. These are more emotionally dysfunctional with negative psychological symptoms. Individuals with PTSD find themselves "stuck" in life and are easily triggered by any of their five sensory nerves.

Some common psychological symptoms of trauma include flashbacks, nightmares, intrusive thoughts, anxiety, panic attacks, fears, obsessive-compulsive behaviours, phobias, depression and other mood disorders, denial, shock, loss of hope, anger and frustration, agitation, avoidance, changes to eating habits, disruptive sleep patterns, dissociation or numbness, inability to concentrate, memory problems, isolation, and hypervigilance.

There are several measurements of traumas, depending on the severity of it. Some can be like a rug burn that takes a shorter healing period, and others can be like a deep cut that causes an infection. Most of us traumatized by deep wounds and infected by neglect can witness negative symptoms. Like a physical cut that is infected, a medical professional will open the wound and explore all the possible causes of the infection. So too, does a professional therapist, who will take time, depending on the severity wound, to explore the rationale for healing to be activated.

Traumas that occur as a single occurrence may not significantly impact the nervous system. Once the incident has been dealt with upon impact, it may be classified as acute trauma or stress disorder (ASD). This can be related to any stress caused by a natural disaster, accident, or abuse. The incident is significant because it affects the individual's mental and psychological well-being.

ASD generally manifests from two to four weeks following a stressful experience. This is more classified as a rug burn. We can share what happened, how it affected us and move on.

Usually, cognitive behavioural therapy works best in redirecting the thoughts to become proactive by doing something and staying positive. To avoid ASD from leading to PTSD, we who experienced trauma should seek professional support. We should expose our trauma by discussing it and getting it out of our system. We must seek medical help to deal with the physical and emotional symptoms if necessary. Physical pain or cognitive issues, including depressive and anxious feelings, are all systems that must be sorted out from the trauma.

It is essential to avoid isolation and unhealthy coping mechanisms such as substance abuse and addictions, gambling, illicit drug use, misuse of prescription medications and self-harm. We should discuss any safety issues, including suicidal or homicidal ideations or self-harm.

Traumas can occur on multiple occasions, the reoccurrence of abusive relationships, financial struggles, job loss, medical and mental diagnoses, motor vehicle accidents and the loss of loved ones. And not forgetting those frontline and first responders who witness trauma and vicarious trauma daily as part of their job responsibility.

When we experience stressful occasions one after the other, like a soldier, police officer, firefighter, nurse, doctor, or ambulance attendant, witnessing injuries, illnesses, and deaths of loved ones, a combination of events can contribute to chronic traumas. And like acute traumas, if not dealt with professionally, it can lead to PTSD.

To avoid chronic traumas from leading to PTSD, any individual who experienced trauma in such measurement should seek out professional support. Professional support like psychotherapy with a treatment plan can help, using evidence-based therapies. Some proven therapies include Cognitive Behavioural Therapy (CBT), Cognitive Processing Therapy, Mindfulness, Diaphragmic breathing, Music Therapy, Exposure Therapy, Visual Therapy, Art Therapy, Spiritual Therapy, and many other healing therapies.

Sometimes, young individuals who grow up with many unpleasant experiences can have similar negative occurrences. Adolescents may believe that this is just how life is. There might be conflict at home; adults argue and get into unresolved disputes in front of their children. Couples are becoming belligerent and pugnacious and failing to provide children with daily necessities, including insufficient food, warm clothing, hugs, words of encouragement, praise, and affection.

Some things are awful in a way that affects young people on the inside, where no one can see. Adults, older siblings, or classmates are speaking negative words. Threats, anger, and making accusations can have a significant impact on a person's life.

Many children and teenagers believe that no one can help them, as they usually blame themselves for what they experienced. They may be frightened, unhappy, or angry most of the time or blame themselves for what is going wrong. Trusting individuals may also be challenging because of letdowns, absences, neglects, and assault.

When we believe that no one cares about us, don't have the proper support around us and have not come to terms with our past, our minds may want us to believe we are responsible. Some of us may think it's our fault, and our thoughts are stuck there. It may lead us to withdraw from others and isolate ourselves.

We may be easily triggered when we hear others with their stories that are similar to ours and carry guilt and shame. We may feel quite different from others and especially if we think we don't fit in. We may feel we are not good at anything, no matter how hard we try, leading us to want to quit. It's easy to lose hope. However, if our finger is above the water of life, there is hope. There is always light at the end of the tunnel, regardless of how dark we may feel.

The treatment of complex trauma is developing as the mental health stigma is exposed. We all have our own experiences and struggle with trauma differently. What coping strategy works for one individual might not work for the next. Also, remember that what works one day may not work the next.

The good news is that more evidence-based therapies are being implemented, showing more significant progress. Every generation has its unique coping strategies that work. Each therapy option aims to give a corrective emotional experience for recovery.

Most experienced trauma therapist uses Cognitive Behavioural Therapy, Cognitive Processing therapy, Eye Movement Desensitization and Reprocessing, Somatic Therapy, Dialectical Behavioural Therapy, Grounding techniques, Mindfulness, Art Therapy, Music Therapy and many others.

Cognitive Behavioural Therapy (CBT) is a type of therapy that focuses on feelings, emotions and behaviours stemming from our thought process. The form of therapy helps individuals to recondition their minds and restructure their thinking. It helps them to connect beliefs, feelings, and behaviours, modifying the negative thoughts to be optimistic.

Cognitive Processing Therapy (CPT) helps understand the causes of behaviours. It allows individuals with traumas to identify the stuck points preventing them from moving forward. There are usually twelve modules to help reframe the mind to put closure to the past. Factors provoking trauma symptoms causing depression, anxiety, and other mental conditions are identified and addressed.

Eye Movement Desensitization and Reprocessing (EMDR) is a treatment that uses gentle tapping (or tones) to help individuals reprocess traumatic situations and establish new beliefs about them. Some individuals find this therapy form helpful, while others prefer other methods.

Dialectical Behavioural Therapy (DBT) is usually recommended for individuals with borderline personality disorder (BPD). Most individuals with this diagnosis experience several traumatic events in their lives and abuse. Their emotional skin is usually thin, like a tomato's skin. They can be susceptible and emotional. DBT helps to understand the functionality of an individual and how to cope. Radical self-acceptance, distress tolerance and mindfulness are a big part of this therapeutic strategy.

Grounding techniques are used to cope with the symptoms of flashbacks, nightmares and intrusive thoughts from a traumatic event. It helps individuals to live in the present. Grounding therapy helps one understand the past and come to terms with the present. Grounding techniques use simple activities, including using a rubber band around the wrist which can be snapped to get the person's mind in the present. Also, sitting under the shower feeling the sensation of the water, dancing, stretching, meditation, deep breathing, journal writing, seeing beautiful sceneries, smelling delightful fragrances, touching soft textures, and tasting tasty things. The goal is to tap into the five senses (touching, seeing, smelling, hearing and tasting) to stay connected with the present.

The root of trauma can stem from any events that had a negative outcome. First responders (police officers, firefighters, EMS workers, medical professionals, and soldiers) are prone to traumatic events affecting their mental and psychological well-being. We all can experience trauma from early childhood from being exposed to situations we are not equipped to handle. Physical violence, emotional and physical abuse, sexual abuse, motor vehicle accidents, physical accidents, and exposure nasty to divorce and separation can have a negative impact on the brain. We must protect the mind from creating negative memory cards that can have long-lasting emotional scars. There are some things we cannot prevent as it may be part of the job responsibility as a first responder worker; however, debriefing and exposing the trauma before it scars the mind deeper can help. The more we think about something, the more the thought is ingrained in the mind, like learning a new language.

Some people have been struggling since the worldwide COVID-19 pandemic. Many individuals have lost their loved ones from the pandemic, leaving fears and anxiety. The continual dread of being ill, the death from COVID-19, and hearing about the deaths of many others continue to create trauma symptoms. The pandemic's confinement in the inability to leave the house, a total loss of control, and tremendous sadness have also resulted in the development of various traumatic symptoms.

Depression and racism can lead to trauma. For people of colour (who are victims of systematic racism and violence), the experience of being continually threatened can lead to trauma and PTSD.

Motor vehicle accidents or any type of other road accident lead to physical traumas and leave a substantial impact on mental health. And if such accidents lead to a disability, it could be the reason behind permanent or long-lasting symptoms resulting in PTSD.

Traumas caused by work-related factors are often left unnoticed. They are triggered by work overload, verbal and non-verbal abuse, hectic schedules, overly strict bosses, low salaries, and other similar factors. Individuals with a micromanager as their boss can cause more damage to the mind of a worker than the boss anticipate. The concept of accommodation is essential to reduce fear, anxiety, and possible trauma to employees who feel they are always under the radar. Like other types of traumas, work-related trauma also negatively impacts mental and emotional health and may result in PTSD if not addressed on time.

Trauma survivors might shift from feeling unique to feeling 'awful,' sad, depressed, lonely, lack of motivation. This self-promotion is an intricate defence against the unbearable sense of being an outsider and undeserving affection. Loss of self-esteem is a common symptom of the negative effect of trauma.

The therapist's responsibility is to assist trauma victims to discover their identity, value, and worth. Self-reflection and getting a person to understand their reality can be a challenge when a trauma victim.

Sexual relationships are usually avoided or accepted when someone has been a victim of sexual abuse. Some individuals may become sexually promiscuous and withdrawn as they live in daily fear. They may force themselves to enjoy sexual pleasure, but it's their go-to.

Survivors of sexual and physical abuse frequently struggle to be in their bodies. Because of this separation from the body, several therapies have been proven to promote trauma recovery, including yoga, mindfulness, and grounding techniques. A vast, overwhelming, unbearable shame often follows trauma.

Loss of trust is a severe effect of trauma. This is particularly true if the abuser is a close relative or friend. When someone you trust harms you, this becomes your 'normal,' it's difficult to tell others as you may feel embarrassed or shameful. However, exposure is the key to preventing others from being abused by the same person.

Trauma survivors will keep recreating the scenario in their minds, hoping to get a different result. This technique is prevalent and can create a negative emotional feeling if the closure is not completed to the traumatic event—anything perceived as an indication can be deceiving, causing reoccurring memory cards to surface.

Personal power is the inner resiliency, strength and agency that resides within each individual. It is the ability to assert oneself, make choices, and take action in alignment with one's values and goals. In the context of the recovery process, personal power plays a crucial role in rebuilding one's life after trauma. However, it is essential to acknowledge that trauma can significantly impact an individual's perception of personal power.

Trauma can potentially shatter a person's sense of

control and autonomy. It can leave individuals feeling helpless, powerless, and stripped of their agency. The experiences of hurt, abuse, and trauma can create a deep-seated belief that they are fundamentally flawed or unworthy of asserting themselves and making choices. These disempowering beliefs can further perpetuate a cycle of victimhood and hinder the healing process.

Reclaiming personal power involves challenging these disempowering beliefs and recognizing that trauma does not define one's worth or capabilities. It requires a shift in perspective, acknowledging that the trauma was an external event that happened to them but does not have to define their identity or future. It involves taking responsibility for one's healing journey and reclaiming the power to make choices that lead to personal growth and well-being.

In the aftermath of trauma, it is common for individuals to underestimate their resilience and strength. However, it is essential to acknowledge that resilience is an innate quality within each individual. It is the ability to bounce back from adversity, adapt to challenging circumstances, and thrive in adversity.

Exploring the innate resilience within individuals who have experienced trauma involves recognizing the courage and strength they have demonstrated throughout their lives. It means acknowledging the countless times they have faced adversity and found ways to persevere. By reflecting on past experiences, individuals can understand their inherent resilience and draw inspiration from their triumphs over difficult situations.

Identifying personal strengths is another crucial aspect of rediscovering personal power and resilience. Each person possesses unique strengths: resilience, compassion, creativity, and determination. These strengths can serve as sources of empowerment, reminding individuals of their capabilities and that they have the inner resources to overcome their challenges.

Cultivating resilience involves engaging in self-reflection and acknowledging personal growth. It means recognizing and celebrating the progress made along the healing journey, no matter how small. Positive affirmations can be powerful tools in reinforcing a resilient mindset, reminding individuals of their strengths and abilities. Embracing challenges with a growth mindset, and viewing them as opportunities for learning and growth, can further cultivate resilience.

By understanding personal power, recognizing the influence of trauma, challenging disempowering beliefs, exploring resilience, identifying unique strengths, and cultivating resilience through self-reflection, positive affirmations, and embracing challenges, individuals can rediscover their strengths and reclaim their power. This process of self-empowerment and resilience-building is an essential part of the recovery journey after trauma, allowing individuals to move forward with confidence, purpose, and a renewed sense of worth.

Trauma profoundly impacts our sense of self and how we perceive ourselves in the world. When we experience hurt, abuse, or trauma, it can significantly shape our self-perception and identity. The wounds inflicted upon us can lead to shame, guilt, and worthlessness, distorting our understanding of who we are at our core.

In the aftermath of trauma, individuals often face common challenges in their identity development. They may struggle with a diminished sense of self-worth and a loss of trust in themselves and others. The trauma can redefine their identity, casting them into the role of a victim or survivor, and this narrative can become deeply ingrained. It can be challenging to break free from this identity label and find a new sense of self that goes beyond the trauma.

However, it's essential to acknowledge that identity is fluid and has the potential for positive growth and change. Redefining our identity after trauma requires intentional and compassionate effort. Cultivating self-acceptance and self-compassion is a vital first step. It means embracing ourselves, scars and all, and recognizing that we are not defined solely by our past experiences. By extending kindness and understanding towards ourselves, we can begin to heal the wounds inflicted by trauma and foster a more positive self-image.

GENERATIONAL

TRAUMA

To be born, we need 2 Parents, 4 Great Grandparents, 8 Great-Grandparents, 16 Second Great-Grandparents, 32 Third Great-Grandparents, 64 Fourth Great-Grandparents, 128 Fifth Great-Grandparents, 256 Sixth Great-Grandparents, 512 Seventh Great-Grandparents, 1024 Eighth Great-Grandparents, 2048 Ninth Great-Grandparents. To be born today from 12 previous generations, you needed 4094 ancestors over the last 400 years.

Think for a moment... How many struggles? How many battles? How much ambition and desire? How many love stories? How many expressions of hope for the future are you living in now? How many years are spent working to make tomorrow better? We inherit much more than meets the eye, including our family's emotional heritage. The concerns, fears, prejudices, phobias, and more of our parents or grandparents are frequently transmitted to us through their behaviours, cultural norms, and even our genes. Are you still in any doubt about being a product of your ancestors?

One of several risk factors that can lead to mental illness is genetics. And unresolved traumatic events can develop a pattern in our minds from our parents and the generations before us, creating hatred and dislike for specific places, things and people.

Our genes are the blueprint for our bodies and brain growth, passed down from our parents and ancestors. Mental illnesses, like genetics, are very complex. No specific gene predicts whether we may develop a mental disorder. For example, even something as basic as our eye colour is affected by up to 16 separate genes! Instead, many genes influence how our brains develop, making us more or less likely to develop a mental disorder later in life.

Mental illness can run in families. Those with a mental disorder in their family may be slightly more prone to develop one themselves. Mental illnesses, on the other hand, are not solely a result of heredity. Both genetic and environmental variables have a role in their development. Mental illnesses may stem from traumatic events our ancestors went through to survive. Their way of survival was not putting closure, which got transferred to the generations after them.

Notably, individuals who have inherited DNA variants that put them at risk don't always get sick. Other variables, biologically protective and bestowing resilience, are assumed to be involved in deciding whether an individual remains healthy or develops a psychological illness. And with this, we also need to consider the environmental influences that interact with gene activity. The nature of these moderating elements is still a mystery.

So what is Generational Trauma? An easy way to understand generational trauma is to relate it to the fact that we inherit physical and psychological characteristics from previous generations. Physically we inherit body type, height, hair, eye and skin colour. Psychologically we inherit behaviours, gestures and how we process information. Cognitively we could develop what we consider "normal," that is, everyone's "abnormal." We need to know how we think about things, how we process information and how we behave is considered "normal" in our society.

Family and environment form many of our personalities, including our interests, hobbies and core beliefs. And it's not just limited to the immediate family, but the influence comes from a generation of grandparents. Each adult passes on their knowledge through their own experiences to the children. It makes sense that we learn from our past, but what can we learn from our family history with unresolved traumas can have a long-lasting negative impact on us.

Generations can transmit genetic or epigenetic traits from emotionally charged and stressful events. This can have a significant impact on our lives by increasing our susceptibility to a variety of mental health disorders. Some of us, who may never have a history of trauma, can easily be triggered by vicarious trauma or traumas that may not significantly impact others. This may result from their family generation, who had experienced some trauma and was passed on but stayed dormant.

Common symptoms we can experience and may not know where it's coming from include depression, anxiety, low self-esteem, dissociation, hypervigilance, shame, or guilt. It may be a good idea to find out if there is ancestral trauma.

The trauma responses we experience can be rooted in past experiences instead of what we encounter presently. Maybe you weren't abused growing up, but your parents or grandparents were. Perhaps you didn't face discrimination or live through a war, but your great-grandparents did. We all have different responses to stress and traumatic events. The typical symptom is our response to fight, flight, or freeze. There are nuances of each different response, including hyper-independence and people-pleasing. What happens during those stress responses may be related to intergenerational trauma and can affect our mental and physical wellness.

Families with a history of unresolved trauma, abuse, depression, anxiety, psychosis and addictions may continue to pass on maladaptive coping strategies and pessimistic views of life to future generations.

Descendants can be influenced by trauma that their parents or even grandparents witnessed. It is possible for the trauma experienced by the first generation of survivors to be passed down through multiple generations via mechanisms associated with post-traumatic stress disorder (PTSD). For those who haven't had to face the traumas of previous generations, the next generation may be trapped in "survival mode" since they've been taught how to avoid those hazards in the future.

Historical trauma is closely related, as it is intergenerational trauma experienced by a specific cultural, racial, or ethnic group. Groups targeted or oppressed historically through genocide, enslavement, or language bans, may suffer from the effects of historical trauma. It is not unusual for people to be affected by past and present trauma.

When traumatic experiences co-occur and are compounded by one another, they may have a detrimental influence on one another. Generational trauma can affect us all; those at the highest risk are in families that have experienced significant forms of abuse, neglect, torture, oppression, and racial disparities.

Studies have explored the effects of transgenerational trauma on Holocaust survivors, the Khmer Rouge killings in Cambodia, the Rwandan genocide, the displacement of American Indians, and the slavery of African Americans, among others. There is a higher rate of anxiety, depression and PTSD in trauma survivors and their children. The root of the triggers can lead to the past more so than the present.

When parents live under oppressive circumstances (my grandmother shared some stories), they develop "survival messages" (like "don't ask for help, it's dangerous"). Some people may have been taught similar strategies, passed on from generation to generation. While these messages may have helped protect earlier generations, they can cause later generations to have a fearful and distrustful outlook on life. In addition, it can create fear of seeking professional support, further alienating the necessary support to overcome the aftermath of the trauma itself.

Anyone can experience intergenerational trauma. People from marginalized groups, including people of colour and those in lower socioeconomic classes for generations, may have more pronounced experiences with intergenerational trauma. Those descendants of people who have experienced violence from living in war zones and other hardships (World War II, the Cold War, the Vietnam War, or conflicts in the Middle East) may be more likely to experience intergenerational trauma.

Historical trauma was first discussed concerning survivors of the Holocaust and their descendants. But this type of intergenerational trauma also affects many other groups of marginalized communities, including Japanese Americans with ties to Japanese internment during World War II, Black and African American people, those of Vietnamese and Cambodian descent, Australian Aboriginal tribes, and those belonging to North and South American Indigenous tribes, mainly descendants of the Indian Reservation Schools in Canada and the United States.

Some experts in the medical community attributed intergenerational trauma to the stress of living with a traumatized person who may still be reliving horrific events. Others attributed intergenerational trauma to children becoming "containers" for their parents' unwanted pain.

Developing countries like India, which the British colonized and have been through communal uprisings because of colonization, also experience intergenerational trauma. The impacts of caste-based trauma can be readily evident. Baba Saheb's Mahad Satyagraha in 1927 shared about caste-based trauma. My grandmother shared about this as she and her family were from caste-based trauma. She shared about the partition of India and the 84 Sikh Genocide, the Babri Masjid Riots, and the Taj attack.

Our history of ongoing collective distress means that this suffering is often "forgotten" to us. Trauma often goes unrecognized because it is suppressed and projected onto children. We've passed it down through the years like a family heirloom. As a result, mental illness is on the rise. It's not or shouldn't be our legacy.

Intergenerational trauma isn't something that can be easily pinpointed. It is often covert, undefined, and subtle, surfacing through family patterns and forms of hypervigilance, mistrust, anxiety, depression, issues with self-esteem, and other negative coping strategies.

Traumas significantly affect the immune system and may contribute to the generational curse of autoimmune diseases and other chronic illnesses. Trauma contributes to poverty, compromised parenting, diminished attachment, chronic stress, and unstable living environments, directly impacting children and their development.

Intergenerational trauma can bring some families closer emotionally, causing others to drift apart. Intergenerational trauma might affect families in many ways, including disconnection, denial, detachment, distance, and impaired self-esteem. Traumas stemming from the depreciation of a person's life experiences, compared to generational trauma, can create trauma bonding or an emotional connection.

An individual who has undergone trauma tends to have elevated anxiety levels. The ability of anxious parents to teach their children to self-soothe can be diminished. Intentionally or not, they may also indicate that the world is dangerous. This can then lead to unhealthy coping mechanisms.

Traumatized individuals are more likely to develop depression, and depressed parents may not be as available to their children as they would like. Children may feel neglected if they are required to care for themselves in ways that are not age appropriate. The phenomenon of dissociation is widespread as a coping mechanism for trauma survivors. This is characterized by the separation or division of mental processes through which the effects of trauma might be transmitted. There is a disconnection between thoughts and memories; individuals may feel numb and detached from their bodies.

Generational Trauma effects can be transmitted through conditioned response or learned behaviour. This is especially common when there is a lack of alternate role models. An individual with poor parenting skills may repeat the same destructive habits, even when a child wishes to do things differently. Parental modelling is hugely influential. Parents teach their children coping techniques, communication styles, and boundary setting, among other skills. This is passed on to the next generation.

Intergenerational trauma in families can perpetuate unhealthy tendencies. Trauma bonding frequently occurs in settings where abusive behaviour alternates with moments of positive attention and caring.

There is a need to break traumatic attachments.

The more trauma our parents and grandparents experience, the more likely we will react negatively to stress. Trauma can also impact microglia, the cells in the brain and central nervous system that compose most of the immune system.

During trauma, the microglia in the brain go haywire, causing sadness, anxiety, and dementia. This can lead to genetic alterations that can be transmitted to future generations.

Decades ago, there was no recognition of genetics' role in mental illness. People who suffered from addiction, anxiety, depression, and other mental disorders were misdiagnosed, maltreated, and ultimately blamed for not behaving how society wanted them to. Psychological research on the relationship between human experience and the psyche has brought a clearer picture of what was labelled a generational disease.

We need regular discussions about mental health and the effects of generational trauma. Gen Z is a leading example in their efforts to normalize therapy, have painful talks with family members, and advocate for universal access to mental health care. Raising awareness and eliminating destructive cycles is vital to break the intergenerational bondage of trauma.

The dearth of information and social stigma surrounding generational trauma has cheated many of us from understanding why we struggle the way we do and the cause behind our behaviours and beliefs. Many individuals take the initiative to learn how to deal with their mental health issues because they're growing up in a period where access to mental wellness is more readily available.

Breaking the cycle of generational trauma begins with identifying and tracing its roots. Generational trauma occurs when the effects of a traumatic experience are passed down from one generation to the next. It's possible that we didn't witness the original trauma, but we're still dealing with the after-effects of it.

Mistrust is a significant obstacle to resolving generational trauma. A skeptical attitude can be carried down from generation to generation if these messages are heeded in the present. There is a need to feel safe, protected, heard, and understood.

Untreated trauma can lead to dysfunctional methods of bonding and coping, which may appear normal. When multiple generations are harmed, this is even more prominent. Many of us may not realize the impact of generational trauma. It takes time and perseverance to heal the wounds of past generations.

As much as traumatic experiences can be passed down from generation to generation, the ability to overcome trauma follows the same pattern. We can build resiliency. Open and loving communication styles between generations helped foster resilience and connectivity. Healing can occur when survivors of trauma openly tell their stories and when descendants can deal with their parents' traumatic past.

We can view the world differently when core beliefs are muddled with our generational mistrust, doubt, resentment and insecurity. Our ability to trust others can be hindered. This affects relationships and the development of a healthy sense of self-worth.

Someone with inherited trauma must be reminded that recovery can be ongoing until proper closure to the past. It's important to note that healing intergenerational trauma often looks different for everyone. As with any healing or intervention, there is no one path to healing intergenerational trauma and no definition of what it means to heal. Acknowledging the validity of the trauma and where it comes from is an essential step in adequately holding space for healing.

ABUSE

Abuse includes anything that we did not permit to our being. This may consist of the infliction of pain, a punishment that causes bodily hurt, unjustified confinement, intimidation, mistreatment, discomfort, and suffering from someone or something. This may be perpetrated verbally, sexually, physically, spiritually, or mentally. We all have been a victim of abuse from time to time. However, certain levels of severity of abuse leave a so-called negative 'memory card.'

The severity of abuse carries emotional pain affecting us mentally and psychologically. Some of us have been abused as a child, as youth, adults or even as an elder in the geriatric population. Perpetrators of abuse can be anybody, including family members, friends, neighbours, colleagues, bosses, and others we respect. We must move forward and bring healing. Otherwise, the abuse will affect us in the future. So many of us suffer from maintaining healthy relationships because of being abused. To move on with our lives, we must address the issues, the cause, the effects, and the solutions.

There isn't just one reason why abuse occurs; several contributing factors must be considered. Abuse occurs in most, if not all, of our lives and can begin as early as childhood. When individuals have an early childhood experience of abuse, they can grow up thinking it is normal behaviour. Some parents have abused their children verbally and physically because of cultural upbringing. Some individuals have abused their spouses in all forms, just as they witnessed growing up in their homes. Then some children use their adult parents as they live with an entitlement attitude from what they pick up at school, on social media, or with their friends.

Some parents who abuse their children have abused themselves and use that as an excuse, claiming they did not know better. Some people have sexually exploited their children or the next-door neighbour's child through what started as engaging conversations at their workplace, getting involved with pornography, or trying new things.

Some negative impacts of abuse include mental health issues, depression, anxiety, and psychosis, which leads to unhealthy coping strategies such as substance abuse and addictions, gambling, poor eating habits, weight gain, illicit drug use, misuse of prescription medications, sexual promiscuity, self-harm, and suicide and homicidal ideations.

As mentioned earlier, in many cases, the abused individual can become an abuser. Stress, PTSD, eating disorders, and other disorders also evolve from abuse.

Abuse can lead to cultural disconnection because of shame and embarrassment. In adults, abuse can lead to financial instability, issues staying at one job or trouble finding a career that brings happiness. It can also cause some to have a limited social life or marital and relationship problems. It can also lead to a lack of motivation and cause personality disorders to develop, like narcissism.

Several types of abuse affect us psychologically and mentally. We must understand that it becomes difficult to remove once the mind is scarred and 'memory cards' are formulated without proper support. When we know abuse, we can understand its impact on our minds and the need to find a suitable form of therapy that can rewire the brain, recondition the mind, and restructure our thinking. Getting proper support in treatment is a tool that works wonders. Working through abuse in therapy is much more fruitful than facing the giant alone.

Physical abuse is an effective form of abuse that happens from as early as infancy. Some infants are physically beaten to stay quiet, which creates a 'memory card' of fear. There are several forms of physical abuse that some of us may have experienced from our early years as a child. Some children have been abused in school by teachers, students, their parents, family members and even next-door neighbours. Some of us have been punched, slapped, had our hair pulled, kicked, choked, pushed, burned, whipped, and belted. All of these forms of abuse fall under the umbrella of physical abuse. Some of us may have had scars, marks, lacerations, fractures, scratches, and unwanted tattoos from physical abuse welts. Since our sensory nerves are connected to physical abuse, 'memory cards' are created, causing post-traumatic stress disorders, fears, and anxieties.

Some of us who have buried the past can suddenly be triggered and feel exposed when watching a movie, hearing someone share their stories, reading an article, or sharing about their abuse.

We must come to terms with our past, put closure to it and move on. Otherwise, it will affect our futures. It is difficult when there are physical scars like having a black eye from punches; burns; lacerations; untreated wounds and broken bones; fractures; or internal bleeding.

We need to get medical attention for physical injuries, just like we need to give attention to our mental injuries. We should not live life in fear; it is necessary that we can replace the 'memory card' that had been created after the abuse with closure to move ahead.

Verbal abuse could be considered harsher than physical abuse as we cannot see the immediate scars visually on the body. Verbal abuse creates long-lasting 'memory cards' that cause individuals to fear like other abuses. We may struggle when a loud noise is present, certain tones are used, or specific language springs into the conversation. We are triggered more regularly when we hear and see traits of abuse. Most verbally abused people suffer from emotional abuse as they can feel demeaned by what is said and how something is said. When we are being told what to do in a harsh and commanding way as though we are being parented, mimicked, manipulated, mocked, called names, gaslighted, ranted at, and insulted, depending on the severity of verbal abuse, some of us may develop fears and anxieties and develop a preference to stay quiet to avoid being shouted at or put down.

Some of us who have experienced verbal abuse may have fixed beliefs that we are being made fun of with name-calling and racial slurs. This is not a proper way to treat another person, even if the names are stated in a neutral tone. Some of us may feel humiliated by negative, sarcastic, criticizing, and mocking words. If spoken words bring shame or embarrassment to us, it can lead to verbal abuse. Being screamed or sworn at, getting a sense of terror and manipulation, feeling threatened or dominated without consent, and being yelled at are all forms of verbal abuse.

To have effective communication, there should always be a speaker and a listener to avoid verbal abuse. Having a discussion, not an argument, is critical to recondition the mind from verbal abuse. The best way to deal with verbal abuse is to avoid engaging in conflict conversations. It does not make sense to engage in any dialogue, which usually leads to exacerbating the abuse. It is better to walk away or advise that once the emotions and behaviours are settled, a discussion can be made to problem solve.

It takes two to create an argument, and we shouldn't fuel the fire when someone is heated and arrogant in carrying a conversation. It's always better to divert the conversation, change the topic or disrupt it by excusing yourselves to the washroom or a phone call. Avoid spiralling a conversation that will bring about a negative result. There is a verse in Proverbs 15 that says, 'A gentle answer turns away wrath, but a harsh word stirs up anger.'

Emotional abuse is another form of abuse that is very common from childhood. Parents, grandparents, schoolteachers, police officers, and others yelling, screaming, humiliating, threatening, harassing, blaming, stonewalling, and calling names can all contribute to emotional abuse.

Emotional abuse could cause us to shut down and become noncommunicative, nonresponsive, withdrawn, helpless, or inactive. Some of us who have been emotionally abused may experience nervousness, trembling, agitation, and anxiety, especially when we are around others who remind us of our abuser.

Some of us may isolate ourselves or be excessively concerned about making sure we are doing the right thing, not to be blamed or yelled at. Our confidence level can drop, and we can endorse low self-esteem to the point that we have others speak for us to avoid being abused. Emotional abuse affects people as much as physical abuse.

When emotionally abused, we tend to become less emotional as a coping mechanism. When we do soul care, we need to do the hard work of reopening our emotions. This can take a lot of time and patience with ourselves.

We need to realize we are safe to process our emotions with ourselves. Again, we need to be kind to ourselves and not speak with the exact words of our emotional abusers when we have an internal dialogue.

Psychological abuse is common today. It causes emotional harm to a person, resulting in fears, anxieties, nightmares, and stress that affect one's mental health.

It takes the form of addressing the elephant in the room, stonewalling, gaslighting, narcissistic tendencies and manipulation. Psychological abuse can develop from traumas and other forms of abuse where an abused individual is targeted purposely by others and is triggered.

Psychological abuse is prevalent and can happen to anyone. Most psychological abuse cases are reported in work, friendships, intimate, familial, and school relationships.

Psychological abuse is as damaging as sexual abuse, emotional neglect, or physical abuse, but unlike other types of abuse, psychological abuse is hard to detect and may go untreated.

Some of us who have encountered psychological abuse may feel unresponsive to our present world, almost as if we are in a catatonic state, as though we are in a coma. We may socially withdraw from others and become highly aggressive, agitated, or irritable. We can be impulsive in our behaviours and can be visibly upset, moody, scared, or nervous. We may avoid certain people and crowds that trigger us or allow our insecurity to manifest. We can also see the desire to have a second opinion to decide anything. This is a negative stamp the brain carries that needs healing; otherwise, it can lead to deep depression.

Psychological abuse can be challenging to identify by ourselves because we can think we are just imagining it. Then we convince ourselves that we are at fault and not the abuser. Therapy is especially beneficial for people who have suffered psychological abuse. We need to rewire our minds to see that our emotions are valid and that we do not deserve to be treated like we were.

Sexual abuse is forcing any form of sexual relations performed without consent. It's an invasion of an individual's sexual organs without permission. Individuals who have been raped, sexually assaulted, inappropriately touched, coerced into sexual contact or forced to have intercourse is considered a victim of sexual abuse.

Individuals who have been sexually abused can

develop fears of having healthy sex. Some men and women live in embarrassment and carry this emotional pain for years. They may feel that being sexually abused by others is their way of sexual fulfillment. Some may become overly protective of their children and siblings to avoid their loved ones from being sexually abused, while other individuals become abusers themselves. Most people who are sexually abused may have the appearance of bruises in the genital areas and sometimes vaginal or anal bleeding when the abuse occurs. This creates a memory card that becomes difficult to let go of. Sometimes individuals may have genital and sexually transmitted infections, which also makes a negative memory card.

The long-term effects include fears and anxiety around sex, difficulty maintaining a healthy sex life, problems having sex without flashbacks and nightmares, and a craving for sexual fulfillment to be rough. They may include preferring similar sexual acts to avoid the flashbacks or thoughts of being hurt if the abuser was of the opposite gender.

To avoid post-traumatic stress disorder, discussing this type of abuse with a professional is essential. There is also a surprising amount of good content in the Bible on healthy sexuality. A significant component of soul care is caring for our physical bodies and feeling at home.

Financial abuse is another growing form, especially among the geriatric population. Some of us may have had finances withheld by our loved ones without access to money or finances. Some individuals may be denied all access to financial institutes and knowledge. Commonly they have no idea how much money they have in their saving account, their assets and investments, as it is withheld by their spouse or significant other. Some elders have been abused financially by their children, who have access to their money and spend it without permission. Some children may have money from the death of a loved one or an inheritance, which has been controlled without permission.

Some of us may have to make tough decisions to break free from being abused financially, especially when we want to work and are told we are not allowed to work by our spouses or significant others. Some of us may be threatened or harassed to quit our jobs; otherwise, our relationship will end. We may not be involved in financial investments or big purchases, and our credit has accumulated, creating a negative credit score. All are common factors of being financially abused which can lead to neglect.

Recognizing if you are being manipulated by someone who controls your money is essential. There is always a choice; sometimes, it may involve the law.

Neglect is considered a form of abuse. Some parents have neglected their children and allowed them to live on the street or be involved with drugs and sex from a young age. They failed to provide the necessities of life for their children. Some children have neglected their parents, mainly older adults and those in the geriatric population who live without proper care, including food and shelter. Individuals with disabilities, including mental health and physical challenges, are sometimes neglected.

Neglect includes not being provided with suitable clothing or being given soiled clothes to wear. Negligence also includes not receiving proper medical care, hygiene, dental, immunizations, and eyewear.

Neglect is also a way to abuse ourselves when we withhold ourselves from our needs. We must address the emotional wounds caused by neglect and remind ourselves of our value and worth.

Lastly, spiritual abuse occurs in any religion by leaders, fellow members, or beliefs. There could be certain expectations that can cause fear and emotional hurt. There could be religious demands with unattainable expectations.

Being told what to do and given an injunction can be spiritual abuse. Some leaders have given a negative taste of faith and religious expectations. Some have used religion to take advantage of people. Religious group members need to be aware not to get caught up in filling an emptiness in their lives by pleasing others without obligations or being forced to.

Spiritual abuse includes being told to believe in religion or spirituality for the sake of a race or culture. We should all be making our own choices without feeling pressured. Some of us who think we are being forced to accept certain morals and ethics that are not in our scope of beliefs or are being restricted to thoughts against what is written in the Holy Books are considered spiritually abused.

Being forced to do things that we don't want to or that are unethical, being manipulated to give donations, and other financial obligations can all be considered spiritual abuse.

To avoid being spiritually abused, we need to make sure we are treated with dignity and respect. We must remember that we are not caught up in using religion as a form of control and manipulation. We need to remind ourselves that we are accountable to others and are not called to harm or hurt others but to support and provide for them. Religious leaders must be mindful that others look up to them for guidance, not to be parented or controlled by opinions and perceptions.

We need to be aware that any form of abuse can scar the mind, and depending on the severity of the scar, the healing can take longer. All forms of abuse leave a negative 'memory card' in the brain, leading to long-term issues. We can address our abuses with professionals who can help create new positive 'memory cards' and put closure to the past.

We need to close the door to our abusive past, as it has the power to prevent us from having a future that can blossom beyond our imaginations. We cannot change the past, but we can change our present and future. We cannot change a person's life choices, but we can change ourselves. We can re-wire our brains, recondition our minds, and restructure our thinking to have a healthy, happy life. This can only be done through emotional healing.

ADDICTIONS

Addiction is a neuropsychological disorder of the brain that drives a person to an extreme and continuous desire to use recreational substances or indulge in unhealthy habits. This provides people with a short-term feeling of 'high,' but addiction is responsible for several severe physical and mental issues in the long term. In simple words, addiction is an intense urge, desire, or dependency on anything that brings about extreme excitement and a burst of good feelings in a relatively short time. But once this 'euphoria' goes away, the person feels lifeless with no energy and motivation to do anything productive. Such people start thinking of themselves as a useless part of society, and to cope with this guilt, they return to their addictions that cause false reality and imaginary feelings of happiness, authority, and high status, and it also wipes away all sorts of worries, guilt, and tension.

The most common addictions most people are familiar with are alcohol and illicit or recreational drugs. However, individuals can be addicted to cyber, sex, shopping, gaming, gambling, and eating. Some people can be addicted to abuse and many other unhealthy stimulants.

Addiction arises when an individual has lost control

over themself. They know something is morally unhealthy and is also damaging their physical and mental health, but still, they can't control themself from going back to that 'unhealthy' thing again and again. Scientists explained that these addictive behaviours are because of the stimulation of a potent hormone in the brain called "dopamine."

Dopamine is a powerful neurotransmitter secreted by the brain's hypothalamus and is responsible for cognitive functions like motivation, pleasure, memory, reward, social skills, and creativity. In short, dopamine is a 'happy hormone' because it makes you feel good.

But in the case of addictions, dopamine is overstimulated and is released in larger and larger amounts. When the addictive stimulus is removed, the average amount of dopamine cannot cause enough pleasure anymore. As a result, stimulation of dopamine-containing neurons becomes difficult through the usual activities that were at first regarded as motivating, rewarding, and pleasurable by the brain.

So, individuals who have an addiction are forced to seek more dopamine by returning to specific habits or substances, which begins the vicious cycle of addiction.

Addiction starts when an individual takes any substance or indulges in any habit that causes a sudden abnormal rise in dopamine, leading to a burst of pleasure and good feelings. And in turn, it activates the motivation and reward centers of the brain. Therefore, when an individual is not taking any addictive things, their brain fails to satisfy the dopamine demands, forcing them to return to their 'artificial dopamine enhancers.'

This cycle continues until the individual develops a

habit of addiction that is very hard to break. If this sounds difficult to understand or imagine, try drawing a process and write down the different parts we've looked at that lead to the point of addiction.

Medical experts classify addictions into three major categories including physical addiction, behavioural addiction, and impulse control disorders. Looking at these categories can help us understand habits better and care better for ourselves and others when they struggle to get complete freedom from this problem.

Physical addiction, also known as substance or chemical addiction, is characterized by physical dependency on a specific addictive substance. This type of addiction is more popular than other types of addiction.

To fulfill physical addiction, one must take specific chemical substances in the body that induce 'euphoria' and detach the person from reality. The standard routes of taking substances include injections or oral.

Examples of physical addictions include alcohol, smoking/tobacco, cocaine, ice (crystal meth), marijuana, opioids, phencyclidine, inhalants, prescription drugs (sedatives, tranquillizers, etc.), and hallucinogens (THC, mescaline, etc.).

"Behavioural Addiction" is equally common as physical addictions. Behavioural addictions will cause an individual to lose control over themself and force them to surrender to those activities that provide a dopamine rush.

This type of addiction is characterized by persistent, destructive attitudes that are compulsive and habitual. Even though a person may look normal physically, it could be that their mind is playing hidden games because it has become addicted to certain activities.

Thus, one must obey their mind's instructions even if they know that the resulting behaviour will cause severe physical, mental, social, financial, or spiritual damage to themselves.

Behavioural addictions include social media, gambling, video games, pornography, sex, food, shopping, exercise, work, pain seeking (as seen in chronic self-harm or cutting), and obsessions (spiritual or to a person).

Impulse control disorders are often recognized as psychological disorders in which individuals struggle to control their emotions and behaviours that are seriously damaging and destructive. Such people exhibit impulses or urge that are difficult to resist. It becomes even impossible in extreme cases, leading to severe addiction or compulsion. It can occur with other types of habits like substance or behavioural addiction.

Impulse control disorder includes Kleptomania, which is a robust compulsive urge to steal things although they don't need them. Trichotillomania is the strong and uncontrolled urge to pull hairs from different parts of one's body. Trichotillomania is regarded as an obsessive-compulsive disorder (OCD).

Gambling falls under behavioural addiction and is characterized by a strong impulse to gamble. Even if gambling causes severe losses, one cannot resist returning to it repeatedly.

Pyromania is a powerful urge to set fires. Health experts believe that pyromania is a way to cope with the prolonged blocking of emotions and anxiety. By setting fires, an individual may feel freedom from anxiety, stress, or overwhelming emotions.

Intermittent Explosive Disorder (IED) is a compulsive, intense, and sudden outburst of raging emotions of anger, aggression, and violent behaviours in response to minor triggers. IED is a mental condition usually observed in individuals from toxic families where verbal or physical abuse and explosive behaviours are expected.

Several factors, including mental problems, issues in professional life, financial situations, childhood traumas, trained relationships, genetics, bad influences, and curiosity, can cause addictions.

One of the biggest causes of addiction is mental and psychological issues. Depression, stress, tension, anxiety, OCD, psychosis, and other life stressors make the brain run out of 'happy hormones.' This is true of people who are not diagnosed and those who know what is wrong when sometimes, even medication is not providing enough relief.

This leads to a high-risk scenario where one develops an addiction to cope with mental distress to feel 'pleasure.' In other words, people with mental health challenges are more likely to seek addictive temporary solutions.

Controlled levels of stress and worries are standard and expected in our workplace. However, when we become overwhelmed, we are more likely to find other ways to escape these situations. Therefore, challenges or issues in our daily lives are the most common social cause of addiction. This usually leads to a series of other unfortunate events.

Unemployment, lack of education, spending more

than one is earning, having no savings, or spending all your money on chronic, life-threatening illnesses could lead to financial instability and dependency. This money crisis can lead to heavy drinking and drug abuse to escape the situation. Gambling is also common in a desperate attempt to fix the problem.

Childhood trauma is another cause of addiction. Individuals who have gone through childhood abuse or trauma are more likely to become addicts later in life. This does not mean that everybody with childhood trauma will become addicted, but it highlights the vital need for making peace with the past.

Strained relationships or a lack of healthy links with friends and family could be another possible cause behind the hard habit of addiction. Boredom or loneliness could lead to binge drinking or recreational drug usage. This could lead to curiosity too. People can have an "I've got nothing to lose" or "it's not like anybody will care" attitude that pushes them to indulge in addictive behaviours.

The genetic factor could also be a potential cause of addiction. The neuropathy created from seeing our parents and others we trust drink can allude to us having that same habit.

Destructive influences are the leading cause of addictive habits. If an individual is surrounded by people who misuse alcohol and drugs or gamble, they are more prone to follow the addiction pathway. In short, our parents, siblings, spouses, or friends directly influence our lifestyle and the development of good or bad habits.

Most individuals, especially youngsters, try drugs or

get into other things out of curiosity. Individuals typically wonder what it would be like to be high and convince themselves they will only try once. And, from earlier, the thought of trying it again and one more every time until it becomes an addiction. A professor once mentioned, "When a man takes a drink, the drink takes a drink, then the drink takes the man." That is a wise statement.

Curiosity is heightened by films and music culture today that makes drugs sound good. Social media and the appearance of being "cool" can be influential.

Addictive habits are a vicious cycle that has harmful and destructive effects. Addiction is the precursor of a destructive lifestyle and declining health. Once an individual start using drugs, drinking alcohol, or getting into similar habits, their life can eventually turn upside down if they are unable to take control or stay sober. It can drastically impact every aspect of their life.

It is usually impossible to live any semblance of everyday life once struggling with addiction. Addiction affects health, finances, relationships and other essential areas of life. Our body, rest, work, dreams, lifestyle, and connection are all affected.

The first and the most critical area of our life that will suffer from addiction is our health. It is ubiquitous in individuals who have an addiction problem and experience a deterioration in their health. This includes short-term and long-term impacts depending on the addiction's type, intensity, usage, and duration. Some of the common health side effects include cardiovascular diseases like irregular heart rate, poor circulation, and in severe cases, even heart attack could occur. Lung diseases could happen, primarily because of too much consumption of alcohol or tobacco smoking. Weakened immunity increases the risk of infections. Liver damage would progress to liver damage in advanced cases.

Addicts frequently complain of nausea, abdominal cramps, vomiting, weight loss, and appetite issues. Addiction could also cause difficulty concentrating and focusing, confusion, impaired memory, and cognitive functioning. It could lead to seizures or a stroke. It has adverse effects on the reproductive health of both men and women. Even death could occur because of overdosing on drugs.

Psychoactive drugs and addictive habits significantly influence our brain's chemistry and physiology. Addiction can lead to depression, anxiety, panic attacks, dependency disorder, and in the long term, hallucinations, delusion, psychosis, and other complicated psychological illnesses. Self-harm and higher suicide rates are also higher in addicts.

After health, it is our finances that are influenced the most by addiction. An individual who loses a lot of money in gambling due to addiction will get back to it again to satisfy their cravings. Moreover, spending money on illicit or recreational drugs, alcohol, shopping, and gaming also threatens financial stability.

Addiction targets our relationships. Individuals always crave something that provides instant pleasure, often ignoring their loved ones. Addiction causes impulsive and aggressive behaviours that lead to abusive traits, violence, and hatred toward friends and family, leading to poor social life and unhealthy relationships. Poor academic performance, unemployment, and having no social life are typical among people who are exposed to any form of addiction.

Addiction, in short, negatively impacts each aspect of our lives. Thus, it is essential to avoid any addiction, even if it is minor or insignificant. Furthermore, these side effects of addiction can lead to a lack of self-control, poor communication skills, and declining mental health that may result in abandonment by your loved ones or, even worse, abandoning them.

If you think you may be codependent on anything that is unhealthy, assess yourself, and get a second opinion before it's too late. Be proactive in making sure you don't create addictive neuropathways. The key is to always be in control of the stimulants that are giving us a dopamine rush. If it is unhealthy, then reframe your mind from entertaining the thought. All it takes is one attempt to become addicted. And most addicts don't see themselves as others see them. Their normal is everyone else's abnormal.

CONCLUSION

Healing from trauma, abuse, and addiction is not a linear path—it is a journey marked by courage, setbacks, resilience, and profound transformation. Throughout this book, we have explored the intricate ways these experiences shape the mind, body, and spirit, often creating cycles of pain that feel impossible to escape. But within every story of suffering lies the capacity for renewal.

As clinicians, survivors, and support systems, we are reminded that change begins with understanding. The willingness to look beneath the surface, to validate pain without judgment, and to walk alongside those navigating their recovery speaks to the power of presence and compassion. Recovery is not defined by perfection—it is measured by progress, self-awareness, and the gentle unfolding of hope.

To those affected: your wounds do not define you. Your capacity to heal, grow, and reclaim your life is greater than the burdens you carry. May the insights offered in these pages serve not only as knowledge but as a bridge toward deeper self-connection and empowerment.

And to the clinicians and caregivers: never underestimate the impact of your attuned listening, your patience, and your willingness to hold space for others. You are the anchors in the storm. The journey continues—but with knowledge, compassion, and connection, healing is not only possible. It is probable.